# Safe

# Sue Boyle

Oversteps Books

First published in 2015 by          Oversteps Books Ltd
                                    6 Halwell House
                                    South Pool
                                    Nr Kingsbridge
                                    Devon
                                    TQ7 2RX
                                    UK

www.overstepsbooks.com

Printed in Great Britain by imprint digital, Devon

*But I have made the step, have quitted the ship of Ulysses;*
*Quitted the sea and the shore, passed into the magical island.*

*Amours de Voyage*
Arthur Hugh Clough
*Atlantic Monthly 1858*

## Acknowledgements

I am very grateful to the editors of *Acumen, Magma, Poetry Ireland Review, Poetry Salzburg* and *The Rialto* in which many of these poems first appeared and to Peter Sansom for publishing others in *Too Late for the Love Hotel* which was one of the prize-winners in The Poetry Business 2010 pamphlet competition judged by the then Poet Laureate, Sir Andrew Motion.

*A Leisure Centre is Also a Temple of Learning*, first published in *The Rialto*, was selected by William Sieghart in 2011 for the Forward Poems of the Decade anthology. It also featured in Cerys Matthews' Radio 4 programme *With Great Pleasure* in July 2012.

My writing has been greatly encouraged by Patricia Oxley; Anne-Marie Fyffe; the Ware Poets; Hilda Sheehan and the Bluegate Poets in Swindon; the Fire River Poets in Taunton; the Corsham Poetry Society; John Richardson; Dawn Gorman; A.F. Harrold; Ernie Burns and Jeremy Sallon who have all given me delightful opportunities to read as a guest at their events.

While I have been working on the poems in this collection, I have also had the privilege of organising the Bath Poetry Cafe and of collaborating with the many excellent poets from across the West Country who belong to it. I have been continually challenged and inspired by their talents and creative energy.

Several of the poems have also benefited from the devoted attention of my Italian translators, Giorgio Piai and Giancarlo Caine from Sacile in North Italy. Working with such dear friends produced many new insights and editorial improvements as well as opportunities for joyful misunderstandings and convivial company. It is a great sadness that Giancarlo Caine did not live long enough to toast the publication of this book.

# Contents

## a few words from the wedding guests

Let him look through the lens of my unforgiving eye;
let solace of surface be denied to him;
let him see too deep; let him see to the heart;
let him see like me,
*said pike.*

Cast her beyond all dream;
may what stirs in her sight be moving bones for her;
may her hunger consume unblinking what it sees;
make her like me,
*hawk said.*

Warn them how weak they are
who can neither melt to water nor hide to air –
they lack my devious brain, my rippling guile;
they are born unwise; protect them,
*otter said.*

Teach them to fillet sweetness from the years
before love locks deathtight on their tardy heels –
they will need to step high and fast in that bloodred dance
while they run with a chance, while their fire flares hot,
*said fox.*

## night thoughts

I lie beside my lover in the dark
but he sleeps in his own world.
Who is he embracing?
What god has he turned to?
Where does he meet his dream?

Our neighbour puts on airs
but my brother says
she leads Gurney's grey horse
from the stables at midnight
and rides the High Street naked.
Stark white as the midnight
and naked as moonlight,
Tom, my young brother, says.

## a leisure centre is also a temple of learning

The honey-coloured girl in the women's changing room
is absorbed in making her body more beautiful:
she has flexed and toned every muscle with a morning swim
and showered away the pool chemicals
using an aromatic scrub and a gentle exfoliant.

She has perfect bone structure: her secret cleft
is shaved as neatly as a charlatan's moustache.
In dreamy abstractedness she moisturises
then spray perfumes every part that might be loved –
tipped throat, underchin, the little kisspoints
below her ears, the nuzzle between her breasts,
her willow thighs.

A bee could sip her.

She is summer cream slipped over raspberries

and so much younger than the rest of us.

She should look around.

We twelve are the chorus:

we know what happens next.

**pavarotti at the grosvenor house hotel**

He ate like one whose happiness was food.
The juice of Thracian pomegranates; bread,
proved overnight and set to bake at dawn;
cheese, apples, a dish of raisins, eggs –
his eyes shone with delight. He was the feast
in every particle, as on stage that night
he would be the music, the music utterly,
and later, she imagined, he would be love.

It was the god in him, to be what he did –
it was his genius. At Wembley, a whole stadium
would be enchanted by his song. She watched him eat
and knew that he was the fire at the heart
of life. He cut the comb, spread it, oozing honey,
on warm bread and asked her name.

Eurydice, she said.

# a place called argentina

Her book says Julius Caesar was murdered here,
where the tramlines end. There are beggars,
police in their *blindati*, foreign priests.
The lovers are new to each other.
It will be their first night in Rome.

Caesar was slaughtered in Pompey's curia
in daylight, by his friends, for the good of Rome.
She will learn to say *buongiorno, per favore*
and gasp 'Alessandro' when he makes love to her.
She believes this love will last.

These pine trees burrow ancient temple floors
to nurture themselves in older, unhallowed earth.
There are warnings to tourists in five languages.
Do not pet the cats. They respond to affection.
They will follow you into the traffic and will die.

There were temples here to the gods and goddesses
of fountains, fertility, the safe passage of sailors,
the good luck of the current day. Now starlings
funnel their black murmurations
in among the pines and disappear.

She imagines the folding of ten thousand wings.
*L'amore. La morte.* How close they are.
The confusion of signs. The fiction of surfaces.

## the magician's wife

He was the best of husbands. At our wedding
the church was almost full.
Mr Cupid had his friend Mr Albert as best man –
matching costumes of lavender silk twill,
pearl buttons, ribbon bindings, white kid shoes.

They did a double act, to produce the ring –
Mr Albert pretending he had forgotten it,
Mr Cupid pretending to be annoyed with him,
all in mime. You have to be respectful in a church.
Then Mr Cupid did one of his scarf tricks
and after a lot of clever business
produced the ring from Mr Albert's ear.
Everyone clapped except the vicar –
I think he was a bit surprised.

They did the photographs outside the church.
Mr Cupid told me when to toss the bouquet –
throw it really high girl, he whispered, high up as you can.
And it went so high, of course, that it disappeared
which was what they'd planned.
While everyone was staring up at the empty sky
Mr Cupid was able to slip away unnoticed –
he had an engagement that night in Manchester.
Then Mr Albert clapped his hands
and white rose petals started falling,
enough for everyone, falling softly, falling very slow,
what the Japanese magicians will often call
*Sky Filled With Summer Snow.*

Everyone agreed it was a beautiful wedding.
Later they changed the faces in the photographs

to make it seem that Mr Cupid had been there all along.
It's a wonder, the new technology.

I never saw his rooms. I never asked.
In summer he had engagements by the sea.
He'd find me somewhere really nice to stay
and meet me every night after the show –
those were our best times.

One night he took me down to the sands
all ribbed and cockled where the tide had been.
The sea was silver in the moonlight;
the air was very clear
and he showed me a boat crossing the bay.
It had an owl and a cat in it, still as obelisks,
sitting bolt upright, staring at the moon.
Their eyes were glittering.

Mr Cupid said, look, they are going to be married,
and I said, they'll be happy for ever after then, just like us,
and he said, yes, and walked me home.

I didn't see him again.

But I have no complaints.

It was a wonderful marriage.

I have had my enchanted life.

## the harpsichord maker of the rue st andré des arts

Did Tobias Schmidt agree
to build the prototype guillotine
because he needed nine hundred francs

to feed his family
or because manufacturing
was his trade?

Had demand for harpischords slackened
or did the order come from a man whom Tobias,
a foreigner, had the wit not to refuse?

Did it matter to Tobias whether he was paid
to shape the *grande barre* of a harpischord
or the crossbar to hold the blade of a guillotine?

the wrest planks for the musical instrument
or the last resting place for the living body,
which was called in the French the *bascule*,

in the English the teeterboard? A woman
comforts a child with a *passacaglia* by Couperin.
Is the harpsichord maker responsible for that?

Tobias tested his new contraption beheading sheep
in the little square where now a smiling waiter
pours us tea from a hammered silver pot.

The husband who left you was an engineer.
He was much happier with his second wife,
you say. He was always chafing to move on.

## ezra jackson and the cat lady

Might I have married her?
The cats were comfortable with me.
I liked her house.

I used to go up to dig the burials
lay each corpse on its bed of straw
and plant a rose.

The first time – so much blossom in the wind
the grass and her dark hair were starred with it,
the earth was easy, that warm moist of spring

but in dead winter, cracking it with a pick
for Old Max One-Eye, Max the Molecatcher –
where did she get such names?

Tabitha Lily, Pantomimus,
Little Bobbins, Empress Valentine –
I asked her if she took them out of books.

*Cats bring their names when they come to you, she said,*
*and take them to their next life when they go.*

I liked the way the fields butted her hedge;
summer, the windsounds in the waves of wheat;
the larks' shrill descant all the long day long
above the deep churr of Gurney's harvester.
She told me the cats competed for her bed.

*Boris the Terrible, my gorgeous boy*
*with that wicked growl on him. He gets there first,*
*but some cold nights I sleep with all fourteen.*

# a portrait of cosimo
*Florence 1519-1574*

What is it, to narrow your eyes
like that against the sun
and a hawk drop down like that
to your outstretched hand
whether she will or not?

What is it to whistle
your hunting hound
and read in those helpless
eyes and hang of head
what fealty is
and what is servitude?

What is it to ride so high
on a horse, thigh
to flank, knee to shoulder,
rein to mouth one music,
melded like lovers,
running in the wind
whether horse will or not?

What is it, to dress like this,
without adornment, all in black
to deal another's death,
to be without conscience,
to be without ill dreams?

*It is to be me.*
*It is to be a prince.*

## the portraits at montacute

From the long gallery they look down on us,
two friends who had believed each other lost

and at four o'clock are still strolling
the green ride with so much to be said.

The volunteers are putting the house to bed
linen, lavender, beeswax, muslin shroud

because moth, dust and miasma do corrupt
as sorrow does, so many being gone.

Sun flares a candle on each window pane.
I would like to have made the trip to Lucca,

Matthew says, but no invitation came.
I think it might be time to give up the car.

If we had met up this morning, Matthew says,
we could have climbed Ham Hill.

From the tall windows, they look down on us –
Burghley, Essex, Monmouth, Dorchester,

the heirs, the hopeful daughters, the good wives,
the sycophants, the terrified, the vain –

and from the safe havens of their gilded frames
they note how slow we walk,

how well we suit the autumn metaphor –
our light on the ebb, our winter on its way.

## new things
*Venice 1849*

So easy to exploit their weaknesses,
these titled strangers, ignorant young men
craving a light they cannot see.

We have the skills, the wit, the varnishes
to cut and reconfigure any canvas
smuggled to our house.

We fray the linen, rub in pumice dust,
fret new gilding with a pouch of sand,
and bury the stretcher nails to bring on rust.

A Bacchus, a dog, a saint we can sell them all,
providing the *craquelure* convinces
and the price is right.

The strangers believe they have purchased taste,
puff up like marsh frogs as they oversee
their trinkets into crates for the journey home.

We hear that fog inhabits the plain houses
where they boast that they outwitted us on price
and order fresh colours for the sombre rooms

to show off their new things.
As if it could be bought,
what we have.

Look at our lagoon, *signori*.
*Luce sull'acqua*. The light of heaven.
The dancing of the water.

## on the road with mr marksbury

A pair of leg irons
dredged from the River Thames
near the Tower of London.
A theatrical crown and a collection
of theatrical hats and shoes.
A bush baby and a golden breasted starling.
A waxwork of George Bernard Shaw
wearing a tweed jacket and plus fours.
A pair of entwined fighting snakes,
two further snakes and a small frog.
An iron shame mask with ass's ears and a candle.
A waxwork of Queen Victoria automated
with a heaving chest and tapping foot.
A german *pickelhaube* leather helmet.
An african elephant.
A boa constrictor.
A red fox.

A gilt-finished swan.
A junior ringmaster's outfit.
A waxwork of a young child sticking out her tongue.
A collection of simulated leather and cardboard hatboxes.
A collection of framed music hall programmes
including Wilfred Pickles in *Hobson's Choice*
at the Grand Theatre, Blackpool and others similar.
A baby rhinoceros.
A wrought iron mantrap.
A half length waxwork of a torso of a young man
with a knife plunged into his chest.
A french executioner's axe.

*Gloria mundi, the dealers whisper.*
*How quickly it passes,*
*the glory of the world.*

**the fine arts graduate tries to sell a painting
to mr marksbury**

What I want to say to her is –

*This reaching out to the barely expressible,
this hunger to find words on the very edge,
this gnomic utterance –*

*I have to sell these things.*

But his use of shadow, she explains,
that otherworldliness which manages to suggest
in the rich, apparently living moment
the countervailing possibility of death.

*He paints too small for the money,
I hear me say. For that sort of money
people want real statement in a room.*

But modesty was his statement, she explains.
The nearest-to-hand subject,
the least 'arranged',
the essential 'is' of things –
these were what he wanted to celebrate.

*This is a painting of lilac.
Lilac is unlucky inside a house.
Lilac is out, I said.*

# mr marksbury's careful choice of beds

From the Camden Town house clearance specialists,
with their stuffed birds, hallstands, cracked majolica
and out of tune pianos –

from the flotsam and jetsam of other shipwrecked lives,
following her divorce, my aunt Irene
furnished her two rooms.

After he closed the shop for the evening, Mr Marksbury
would deliver her purchases, take a glass of port
and reminisce

about the days when totters
could harvest London with a horse and cart
and the pickings if you were sharp –

a nice bit of cranberry, in the better streets
an unchipped piece of genuine Lalique –
but would not cross the hall into Irene's bedroom

though he himself had supplied the figured walnut bed
because that would have been a sure way in his opinion
to lose an extremely good customer.

A shame, he would say quite often to his partner, Mr Paul,
that our friend on the hill has never remarried.
She has an eye for a pretty thing.

## the harlot's progress

She was a greedy suckling, sir, not the timid thing as you've painted her at all. Such mouth on her. Her eyes were ravenous. As a parched throat will have water and the salmon get to the sea, that was my daughter, sir. Your city was in her blood. She ravined for what you had. I knew I'd lose her to the city. I knew it even though I didn't have the wit myself to know what a city was.

Perhaps it was my fault, sir. I knew I was carrying a daughter and I used to say *Life will be good to you my girl. Your mother will see to that.* Meaning that I would love her and care for her, sir, and find her a good husband, a better one than mine. But my daughter didn't want tenderness, nor the kind of life her mother understood. You've drawn her so exactly, sir – those downcast eyes, that bonnet tilted so you wanted to get up close to see more of her pretty face. I dressed that bonnet, sir. I put those ribbons on. Look at the scissors and pincushion hung from her waist as if to say she looked for nothing better in London than seamstress work – it was all a show, sir. The shyness, the nice handkerchief across her bosom, the dainty stepping down into the dirt. Everyone who sees your picture knows the truth about my daughter – what she is, the pleasure to be had from her, the money to be made.

A hawk, sir – his claws are as sharp as rapiers, but when he picks the leveret from the field, it can seem at first that he means no harm. There won't be a mark on the poor creature at the first, nor a puncture in the tender skin. It's only later he rips her, starting at the throat. She was an ignorant, yearning creature, sir, hungry for everything she couldn't have. A gentleman like you with such a power to look down on the rest of us – who else could have warned my daughter when she stepped down from that conveyance – who else, unless you, Mr Hogarth, who must have been standing by?

## the bridesmaids in the strand

They could be lapdancers.
They could be goddesses
waiting in line for the photographer

outside St Clement Danes.
Slender, startling and immaculate
in black *crepe de chine* with boned

and sculptured sweetheart bodices,
they wear high-heeled
Giuseppe Zanotti sandals

in the Cruel Summer design
with crystal anklestraps.
They have come to support the bride.

On the Thames river boat Arcadia,
the wedding party has booked
the full silver service –

goat's cheese panacotta, chargrilled
fillet of salmon, summer pudding
and pink champagne.

Late afternoon –
palaces glide past and penthouses,
monuments and temples to absent gods.

The familiar city is disappearing.
The western river resembles
a roadway of shining fire.

Our bride folds herself like a fan
against the flank of her new husband
and twists the lovely ring.

Her big day is ending.
The bridesmaids have gathered.
She trusts them to see her through.

## a day out on the thames

Even before the paddleboat Golden Eagle
had moved sturdily downriver
from its mooring on Tower Pier,
my grandfather emptied
all his pockets of loose change,
packed off his three disappointing
daughters to the fruit machines
and joined the other men
in the swanky mahogany of the bar.

In the middle morning
they churned past Silvertown
and the Tate & Lyle refineries
which would be destroyed in a night raid
eight years later by the Luftwaffe
but on this day were still choking out
their essential usual smoke.

And then came the bright midday
when the river banks flattened,

the estuary widened,

the land east of the Isle of Sheppey

disappeared

and it dawned on my aunt Irene for the first time –

her spirit reaching out as a migrating bird
might lay its burden of striving for a moment
on an updraught of sustaining wind –

that not only Southend and Clacton
but one day
for a modern girl
all kinds of wordly adventures
might be possible

and almost at once suspected
what in retrospect, she told me,
had indeed proved true –

that this one day –

when the familiar became
so much less important briefly
than the apparent possibilities
of the grey North Sea
and the colossal estuary sky –

that this one day

already occupied the place
it would still hold all the remaining
seventy years of her slender lifetime later –

the best day a cold father's third daughter

would be able to remember in all her life.

## a dressmaking metaphor

Her mother taught our mother. She taught us
to cover plain buttons with fabric scraps,
chalk the right circle for the button's size,
then run two lines of thread, one on the chalk,
the next the needle's thickness further out.
The fabric could be tightened to a mouth:
the dowdy plastic would disappear.

Drab garments came alive. At jumble sales
they found remnants of cloth which had unspooled
on the counters of London stores whose names
they knew well, whose opulence they could sense,
but never saw.

They taught us how to lighten simple days
with what came to hand – patchwork,
walled gardens, old books, evensong,
nurturing fruit trees, taking care of fires,
and that wealth of tales
where any locked door can give way
to a brighter world.

**trust your instincts not your baedeker**

The way to find yourself is to lose the path,
a poet said who went this way before.
In Venice, to reach the island city's heart,
the straight way is the worst. You should ignore

(the poet said who went this way before)
in Venice, as in love, the offered chart.
The straight way is the worst. You should ignore
the sign that points you 'This way to St Marks'.

In Venice, as in love, disdain the chart:
the best way is to choose the unnumbered door.
The sign that points you *This way to St Marks*
distracts you from the gap in the cloister wall.

The best way is to choose the unnumbered door,
the shutter's negligence, the gate unbarred,
the unrecorded gap in the cloister wall:
in seizing the unexpected lies the art.

The shutter's negligence, the gate unbarred –
in Venice, to reach the island city's heart,
in seizing the unexpected lies the art.
The way to find yourself is to lose the path.

**restored**

One day they will make him marvellous again,
the chariot horse whose fragments of statue
wait under this garden laid for a prince.

This oak tree will fall; its tangle of roots reveal
a sculptured eye, the arc of a hoof, the swell
of a polished haunch.

They will replace his armature and speculate –
was this that dangerous tempered horse,
the stallion from the western provinces,

who chafed and pawed the sand at the starting gate,
whose nostrils flared so wide at each tight turn
he delighted all of Rome?

That legend of a horse who grazes now
the night-blue meadows of Elysium
and waits for a kindly groom

to bring news that their sorrow is finished;
they can leave the ignoble city;
at last they are going home.

## scratching the ground

Piranesi imagined prisons under Rome –
dungeons, tunnels, gargoyles, gaolers, chains,
stairways to nowhere,
                    thumbscrews,
                            turning wheels,
broken bridges across the void.

But how lovely the surface is –
setts rinsed by rain now, polished by winter sun,
fountains playing, flowers on the stalls,
these pavement exiles making the day weep
with their accordions, voices, violins, guitars.

So for a season
enraptured by the glory of the flesh
we can forget our hidden histories
but lines are already bitten in the plate.
We will lift the inked paper
from the printing press one day.

                    One day our truths will out.

## time and tide

The Alma in Princelet Street. The Seven Stars.
The Frying Pan. The Crown and Dolphin.
On Stepney Green, The Ship. The Laurel Tree.
The Anchor and Hope at 90 Duckett Street
and The Knave of Clubs. All gone.

My favourite place, the terrace at Rotherhithe.
I watched the new glass city going up – the banks,
the fancy restaurants, the hotels and I asked myself,
what will we look like down here
from one of those shiny towers?
Queer thing to be so far from the river,
like belonging to another world.

In Spital Square, outside Carluccio's,
the girl from Poland is feeding biscuit crumbs
to her little dog and the Chechen boy
is breaking hearts with his accordion.
Towers rise from the rubble of little streets.
Dorset Street. Berners Street. Bucks Row.
We are drinking Prosecco.
It is hot, you complain, so hot.

## appleby

My friend said the Horse Fair will mend your heart
so I took the bus through Temple Sowerby

and Crackenthorpe with my heart's hurting pieces
with my grieving womb

and saw girls like otters in Appleby, boys like eels,
rough, tough, healthy, men and women like acrobats

on each other's shoulders, up up up
the more and the further generations

the strongest rock solid,
the weakest and the topmost unafraid

horses unsaddled, unbridled, unconstrained
in the rush and canter of the river's cold clean water

childless in that exultation of creatures
what comfort could come from that?

## colours

My great aunt, Lily, was born the year
the Whitechapel murder victims died.
She filled her garden with flowers –
fuschias, geraniums, african marigolds –
anything for some colour. One year
she painted the iron railings,
the wicker chairs, the window frames
and the garden bench pale pink.
Another year the paint was all blood red.
Every night, in her dreams, her second boy,
John the rear gunner, who died in a dogfight
over Tripoli, fell down the sky in flames.
All the sisters wore white at her wedding.
Lily told me the wrong things are what last.

## to forget her unfaithful husband

My sister flees to a country
where ancient forests are on fire
and creatures are their own
charred hieroglyphs.

Birds are black bones.
Lizards have shrivelled
in their blistered skins.

This is where I belong, says my sister.
I too am a relic of myself.
The husband I loved did this.
He laid waste to my lovely world.

## another day

Lemons like round bright lamps will gleam
still in their glossy mantle of winter leaves.
The weather contraption will still register
each shift of wind, each change of temperature.
The pond between the clumps of Canary palms
will have this same lazy traffic of golden carp
and ring-necked parakeets
will be swooping and screeching among the trees
the same, but the painted bench
there, by the steps up to the fountain,
where he is reading *La Stampa* now in the winter sun
will be empty. He will have gone.
And I will be the woman whom he loved.

## the sailor's wife

That man's a bit of rough, her neighbours said
the way he swaggers back to her waiting bed
the mess he makes of her cleanly home
his cunning eye.

He sailed into the silence of the snow.
In the space between two breaths, his doctor said
as a ship can slip its mooring ropes too soon
on a too high tide, any heart can fail.

She kept his compass on her windowsill
his boots and walkstick by her garden door
and refused to mourn. A widow is still a wife
she used to say. I am not alone.

To fall from view is not the same as lost.
To journey a different sea is not the same as gone.

## preserving the dynasty

Easy too easy in her narrow bed
she dreams a green garden, dew on dancing feet.
By this day's fail, by fall of this day's night
my dreaming daughter will become a wife.

We braid her hair to take the cobweb veil;
as though the bud enclosed the rose again
a milk-white gown
flowers and floats and flows about her now;
my daughter has become a peerless bride.

Father, priest, husband, black as cormorants,
before the high altar will transact her price –
how thin this band of gold, how much too slight
to sell this daughter, to acquire this wife.

Then she must take the heady wedding wine;
reach the cold knife to cut the offered cake;
pierce the deceptive ice white shell and find
the dark midwinter of her married life.

## dido's lament

My story's simply told. I was the Queen
of fabled Carthage. Nothing now remains
but my sad song. Who would remember me

unless Aeneas, sheltering from the sea,
had charmed me with strange tales?
My story's simply told. I was the Queen,

fierce in my widowhood and chastity,
ambushed by sudden love and then betrayed.
Without my song, who would remember me?

My horses, ships all gone, the great city
I raised from barren sand. No thing remains.
My story's simply told. I was the Queen.

No man in Carthage would have dared to speak
to me of love. A handsome stranger came.
Without my song, who would remember me

and my sad life? It was my fate to be
both pitied and reviled. Love turned to shame.
My story's simply told. I was the Queen.
Without my song, who would remember me?

## the war wife's almanac

In January
she prepared her house for a homecoming –
rosemary, bergamot, thyme in every room.

In February
she knew that her belly contained the world.

In March
she asked her father to make a cot.

In April
the cousins in Back Street received their telegrams.

In May
she looked for comfort among the cows –
the dairy smelt of urine, milk and dung; it smelt of hay.

In June
Charlie Sladbrook came home without his legs.

In July
she dreamt that the earth would lose the moon.

In August
she and her mother bottled the greengages.

In September
she howled her heart out
and named her son Jack after his grandfather.

In October
she learnt to say the word *Passchendaele*.

In November
the troop trains kept going south.
She refused to pray for the welfare of the king.

In December
she said, I have a son.
I am a person who does not give in to grief.

## the death of the emperor

He was harsh and loved: he was feared and virtuous.
Nothing will be the same: nothing will change.
He is not replaceable: he has already been replaced.
He is all his truths and he is none of them
and never was.

Along the northern wall, his soldiers
hear the news and say in their cups,
the emperor was such and such,
or thus and so, what will become of us
will they call us home?

Kites hover in his skies; the fox and wolf
hunt as they always have; women as always long
to be loved by the worst of men.
Sheep wool snagged on thorn;
a half moon in clear sky above the hills
and he who owned it all, indifferent now
being all his selves, and being none of them.

**the visitor**

Who else could have come so softly to this room
have sensed the yearning of my lonely door
or leant so lightly on the air as you?
You could not have come, they said. They knew
so little about love. But I knew you and was sure.
Who else would have come so softly to this room
or leant so lightly on the air as you?

## the return

And if, revisiting, I should discover
the garden just as rich with plum
blossom as before, though some things would be other –

the light bleaker perhaps, the adjacent river
less wanton with its uplights of scattered sun –
and then revisiting you I should discover

your beauty less compelling, it would not deter
me from telling you the reason I had come,
supplicant, as before, but now for something other –

to ask your company through the courtyards, cloisters,
stairways, one by one
as if, revisiting old haunts, we might discover

not the profligate spring and careless summer
we squandered so casually, but, at our later season
something other –

leisured, better mannered, better measured,
owing less to lust this time and more to reason –
as if, revisiting, we might discover
to our astonishment, at last, each other.

## oh my america

The marram grass,
the boardwalk on the dunes,
the lifebelt hung below
the painted sign:

The horizon is not the end.
There is no end.
But you have reached
the limit of yourselves
here
and can go no further.

They stared at the vivid sea;
then crossed the boundary
of the breaking foam
and walked upon the water.

**rilke's fish**

Our torch invents
a walkway through the night.

On the ocean bed, a fish
nibbles its reflection
in a fragment of mirror glass.

All we shall ever know
about the world.

## safe passage

The oculus in the bridge
gives warning that the Tiber
is on the brink of flood.

Thanks to Pope Sixtus and his architect,
the handbag sellers, pampered little dogs,
bravado boys who perch the parapet
and tiny Genghis Khan with his violin
are safe. However high the water,
providing the island
can be seen through the oculus,
to and from Trastevere
the life of the bridge goes on.

If the eye were blinded by water
it would be time to leave
but who can leave himself?

Not John,
the torrent of voices roaring in his head,
nor in their babels, bedlams,
in their fearful rooms,
Janey, Eliza, William, Christopher,
their minds' foundations shifting in the flood,
not these who cry out but none
can rescue from themselves –

as if the drowned could ever cry for help,
fathoms already down
those mountains of blind water.

## pietà

The actresses from the burlesque theatre
have changed from their working clothes
to join the crowds on the pavement
who have gathered to watch
the important procession as it passes by.

Surrounding the popemobile,
dark-suited bodyguards, helmeted outriders,
men with walkie-talkies, armed police.

Now from the hospices, care homes, hospitals,
on crutches, in their wheelchairs, on their beds,
each with a priest or a crisply laundered nun,
the worn-out, injured, fragile, ailing ones
struggle their own slow progress up the street.

Some, as if celebrities for one day,
give us the gracious papal nod and wave.
Some smile. Some cannot smile. Some laugh
as though we wrong-footed motley onlookers
were actors in a lost comedic world.

We do not jostle now, nor photograph.
Clapping and waving fail as each attends
the sorrow and compassion in himself –
the faithless so close to the faithful,
the watchers so close to the watched.

## at sea

*'Souls' in the manifest they used to call*
*ships' passengers and crew. And of that other ship*
*foundered below us, miles down in the dark,*
*'She sank stern first with fifteen hundred souls.'*

Our cruise liner pitched and rolled.
A humbler ship might have broken its back
in the waves and troughs of that April sea.

The decks were drenched, the steamer chairs
flattened, stacked and lashed to the safety rails.
We were in lockdown. Exit doors were chained.

Showgirls lost footing on the heaving stage.
The planetarium juddered its complex cradle
at every tilt. The theatre was closed.

Perhaps he spent his last day in his room.
Perhaps he passed us in a corridor
or shared the glass-sided lift.

For those of us who trusted the great ship,
the towering waves,
watched through thick windows from a height,

were just a spectacle. The man with no future knew
exactly how those waves would gulp him down.
He intended to be swallowed by the dark.

Ship and storm together, their huge noise –
no one on board would hear if he implored
some saviour to undo what he had done.

Soundless the human falling unremarked
while Babylon steamed on – casino, kennels,
shopping, string quartet,

bank upon bank of light –

pounding, churning the fortunate, the saved,
on schedule to their stopover hotels.

*'Souls' in the manifest they used to call*
*ships' passengers and crew. And of that other ship*
*foundered below us, miles down in the dark,*
*'She sank stern first with fifteen hundred souls.'*

## candles for the kursk

*Barents Sea 2000*

Who knows what was lost
when the sea took charge of them?
Who knew them enough to say,
Ignore his name, his rank.
This was the man he was.

Sergei's son, the virgin Nikolai,
black toothed and garlic breathed –
an acrobat in Omsk once looked his way.
Unless with that speechless
airy, supple, spangled girl,
he wanted no truck with love.

Some waited hours, a few waited
days to die. When each is his own
darkness, his memory scrolling,
flickering to its end,
who knows the mystery, terrors,
blisspoints of his years?

This for Vasily, Anya's favourite son,
student of orchids, shore leave stargazer,
who laughed and drank too much
and slept too lightly, afraid in a deeper sleep
to dream again
the black, the mass, the patience
of that water.

## the roman soldier explains things to his son

Beyond a certain point we believe
that a fallen body is not sensible
so we will not experience earth's
tidy and purposeful depredations –
the tap touch of its insects,
the probe of mandibles, or
in the case of a drowning,
the enquiries of little fish,
the resolve of the battening eels.

Whatever the case, nothing to fear
is the way you must think of this.
We expect not pain, but a sense of wonderment
as the body passes itself into the fabric
of these thousand lives of which, before,
it had lived in ignorance.

Who becomes an ant
becomes one of the world's most admired minutiae;
who becomes a fish
will be as astonished as one who travels to the moon;
as a worm, the womb of the earth opens to him again;
as a bird, he will master the over-arching sky.

It does them no favours, the pomp
and circumstance we accord our generals –
the orations, the wailing women, the catafalques.

The dead make their own way to immortality.
Return to earth is the way you should think of this.

## last winter

Delicate and fastidious as young deer,
every night through the hardship of that snow
foxes from Bishop's Down
braved the white floodlights of the lawn for bread
thrown from a dozen windows every day
to feed the birds.
What a wonderful gift, you said,
foxes in a town on show like this –
My window has the best view in the house:
I shall always remember this.

The Greeks had skills to see
the circling predators of the zodiac
against the imagined overarch of stars.
If I had known what you already knew –
that your *always* meant only January to June –
it would not have been the foxes that I watched
but how the mighty hunter was watching you –
glittering Orion, tireless tracker-down
towering above our little block of flats
with Great Dog and the Little Dog closing round.

## together we get the news from oncology

Too late for us now to journey to Bhutan,
to strip the flab and nonsense from our bones
by tracking rare creatures in the imagined rigour
of that thin air.

Those places which sang so richly from the page –
Alexandria, Svalbard, Chiang Mai, Cameroon –
will stay just names to us. We will not learn
what clots the Sargasso Sea, nor what these smell like –
patchouli, bougainvillea.

We talk about the snow leopard
who has come to the end of her species' time on earth
but still extends herself on the mountain ledge
as if this one cold day in this one cold sun
were the beginning of the world.

She has grown from this rock
and still belongs to it.
She is our model how not to be afraid.

## last things

Choose the right person
to take care of your psaltery –
Janet from the house
at the end of Partridge Lane
who will never marry but is
still hopeful she will find love.

Write the post-it notes –
where to find
the birthday book,
the key for the music box,
the nasturtium seeds,
the unopened marmalade.

Choose the right moment
to wave almost gaily from the bed
as if to say, 'now I am quite myself
but the expected change is coming.
This may be our last
uncomplicated day.'

Forgive your enemies
and also those
who have not succeeded
in loving you well enough.

Now take the grey horse, Dreamer,
while dark still haunts
the thickness of the trees
ride up the ridge and look –

those few miles
to the softening horizon,
those few steeples,
those few nestled roofs
are all there is,
are all there ever is.

## at the hospital

It is our turn today.
Our friends are kind
but glad
as if this thing
can only happen
in any one house
on any one given day.

They feel more safe
because more safe than us
savour their happiness
because we are here
because we are at this pass
they are more aware of clocks
how light diminishes
from zenith to the last
of the precious day.

Their talk is gentle
they remember making love
take out their photographs
what lovely things have been
tidy their houses more
tenderly than usual
for the night.

We are deep voyagers to them
already on our way
to a distant world.
A nurse brings tea in a fat mug
two shortbread biscuits
wrapped in cellophane
and checks your drip.
She knows. Our friends know.
Everybody knows.

## views from the bridge

*one*
The Canada goose rasped on the river embankment
like a blunt ripsaw fighting through green wood.
This was a wild creature who had lost its mate.

Every morning we passed and we did not speak of it.
One day one of us would wish
we had the brass neck to noise off like this.


*two*
The way this river cannot be divided
but circumvents what tries to hinder it
and remains one thing.

The way an ocean is always just one water –
a blade cannot sever it nor can you break it
with any blow.

So it seemed to me when I had your love.

### thinking about the swans

Colour is a lesser thing than light:
no bird's gaudy can compete with the white
of swans. Absorbed in their own loveliness
they glide as if they knew a world more fine
than this, their heads inclined
not in the search for food but in a kind
of graceful prayer. Those who paint angels choose
to wing them like swans as if to prove
how close and familiar heaven is
but here is an older thought –
like white swans flying into falling snow
our dead will abandon us; their wingbeats grow
fainter, then vanish. They will become
part of the sky's thick silence and be gone.

## my lover tells me about the emperor's nightingales

The Emperor Maximilian's home was in Mexico, but his heart was in Europe in a squat white castle on a cliff north of Trieste. The tangled woods and shrubland of the karst rose so steeply behind the building that they formed another cliff which morning and evening was alive with nightingales.

Miramare Castle is ugly if your eye for Italian architecture has been trained to love Palladio. A preposterous combination of gothic and baroque – too many windows, too many balconies, too many balustrades – and indoors so darkly panelled and decorated that the classical spirit can hardly breathe. But Miramare was not part of Italy. In 1867 this was Hapsburg Austria, a heavy-spirited, over-bearing empire weighed down by self-importance and pomposity.

Maximilian designed Miramare for himself and Carlota, his beautiful young wife. They adored each other. They planned a perfect rose garden. When Maximilian was ordered to Mexico, homesickness for the clumsy white castle consumed his soul. Young, foolish, romantic, and insensitive, the new Emperor lit on something truly shocking to slake his yearning for his home. He sent back an order for his estate staff to capture two thousand nightingales from the karst and ship them across the Atlantic ocean to assuage his heart with song.

Who organised the capture? Designed the cages? Rejoiced in the chance to manufacture them? Which imperial ship was appointed to be this travesty of an ark? Fortunately for the birds, in an unusually tender quirk of history, before the arrangements for transporting the melodious harvest were complete, Maximilian fell victim to the hot-headed wrangling of Mexican politics, was taken prisoner, tried for the crime of being who he was, and shot. Life engineered the reprieve of her Illyrian nightingales.

*So if you ask me what love is, she writes, I imagine a keeper carrying a cage towards the fringes of a wood. He sets it down on a gravelled path, lifts the latch, eases the door and lets the birds fly free. The release of nightingales at Miramare. That is what love is.*

# there's a story in everything

*That sounds like the beginning of a story,* my sister said.

*You cannot inhabit another person's story.*
Do you remember when sea fog closed the island? Night and
day the fog horn bellowed into the void. A boat had not
returned. Birds huddled on branches. Hard surfaces bleared
with rime. Until that landing there would be no rejoicing, no
going forth. The islanders shunned us. We had no place in
their story. We intruded on their dread.

*Place and time*
I was travelling to the city in search of a better life. The road
dropped into a valley. Sheep on the hillsides. A crossroads. A
church. Meadows, tidy barns, a river fringed with willows,
running water glinting between stones. But I did not know
how to stop. There is only one moment to enter a new story.
If you miss the essential turning, there is no going back.

*The story teller's tale*
No sooner had Odysseus trusted his fleet to the deep water
than the god who hated him stirred up a storm. His ships
were driven further apart every minute in the howling. The
black sky unburdened its pent up waters. Which anger came
up from the sea, which fury came down from above no man
on any of those drenched and tossing vessels had time to
wonder, or could have known. Odysseus was twenty years
wandering islands and landfalls – twenty years until his eyes
rested again upon his father, his dog, his wife, his old nurse,
his dining hall, his son. Story after story Odysseus had to live,
but he was a lover of stories. Would he really have preferred a
clear voyage home on a tranquil sea?

*Which story will you choose?*
Your plane at the end of the runway is a bird on the brink of
flight. You have already imagined the clouds which will baffle
your ascent and relinquished your loyalty to this particular
piece of earth. Suppose the pilot offers you a choice – you can
proceed without possibility of return to a marvellous but
unspecified destination, or you can reclaim your baggage and
go home? Who will you be? Which story will you choose?

*That sounds like the beginning of a story,* my sister said.

Oversteps Books Ltd

The Oversteps list includes books by the following poets:

David Grubb, Giles Goodland, Alex Smith, Will Daunt, Patricia Bishop, Christopher Cook, Jan Farquarson, Charles Hadfield, Mandy Pannett, Doris Hulme, James Cole, Helen Kitson, Bill Headdon, Avril Bruton, Marianne Larsen, Anne Lewis-Smith, Mary Maher, Genista Lewes, Miriam Darlington, Anne Born, Glen Phillips, Rebecca Gethin, W H Petty, Melanie Penycate, Andrew Nightingale, Caroline Carver, John Stuart, Rose Cook, Jenny Hope, Hilary Elfick, Jennie Osborne, Anne Stewart, Oz Hardwick, Angela Stoner, Terry Gifford, Michael Swan, Maggie Butt, Anthony Watts, Joan McGavin, Robert Stein, Graham High, Ross Cogan, Ann Kelley, A C Clarke, Diane Tang, Susan Taylor, R V Bailey, John Daniel, Alwyn Marriage, Simon Williams, Kathleen Kummer, Jean Atkin, Charles Bennett, Elisabeth Rowe, Marie Marshall, Ken Head, Robert Cole, Cora Greenhill, John Torrance, Michael Bayley, Christopher North, Simon Richey, Lynn Roberts, Sue Davies, Mark Totterdell, Michael Thomas, Ann Segrave, Helen Overell, Rose Flint, Denise Bennett and James Turner.

For details of all these books, information about Oversteps and up-to-date news, please look at our website and blog:

www.overstepsbooks.com
http://overstepsbooks.wordpress.com